Other poetry collections
by Stewart S. Warren:

Shape of a Hill
The Weight of Dusk
Second Light
The Song of It
The Sea Always Near
Just One Leaf
Atogaki
Follow Hawk
Friend
Here There is Also Burning
Rehearse Nothing
Great Storms Making Ready

www.heartlink.com

Somewhere Beautiful
Like Earth

Mercury HeartLink
www.heartlink.com

Somewhere Beautiful
Like Earth

the rest of the poems from 2012

Stewart S. Warren

POEMS

RENEWAL DIRT

WHAT NEED OF FOREVER

YOU'RE SOMEBODY'S BLUE

Introduction

It's already old: that eastern hurricane and southwestern draught, this year of flag waving and attempted secessions, these poems and myths by which I've lived. Already non-existent, those clever headlines burn quickly and quietly now like mist in the rising sun. It's Friday morning. In a couple hours, Yoga and the consistency of a practice that reveals the fluid and mutable nature of this Great Moving Mystery. And the sun, for the first time since Summer Solstice, is arriving a minute earlier—it's December 21st, 2012.

This morning I woke a little after 4:am from a dream in which an adversary queried, "Tell me, how did I hurt you?" I searched and searched but could not find the injustice, the moment of attack. It was not there as it had always been. There was no attack—that's the truth, the freedom of it. For an instant I thought I might need that story and the perceived protection it could provide me from *future* wrong doings. But the nakedness I felt was not uncomfortable, so I breathed into the pose and found a spaciousness there, a further opening. Simply, I experienced the unemotional fact of our unity. Then some words followed: *There is only one of us here.*

I have written those words, and lines like them, often enough that they are slowly becoming a working part of my mind. Or perhaps, more correctly, the emerging truth and transformation, which is this miraculous flowering from nothing, has found me here, reticent and stubborn as I often am. And I am relieved that my thoughts are not original and reassured by knowing that this wave of Reality is coming through you, too. The idea of being separate and alone is part of the old myth, and at this moment it seems like a very silly thought.

You might wonder why some of the poems am I'm presenting in this last collection of 2012 contain perspectives that I admit are passé. Hmm...because I can't not express myself? That's as good a reason as any. And when I apply half of a favorite paradox—*My life is none of my business*—I could let it go at that. (The other half, by the way, has to do with absolute responsibility.) But here I find myself returning to one of the central themes of my life: *I am here to witness.* And, as I've shared before, I'll be making my report later, though I'm not sure this reporting happens here in the world as we think we know it.

So witness I have. This collection, not too different from my other books, explores some personal history, points a cautioning and critical finger at certain constructs of society, questions our footing in so-called reality, and speaks to, and from, that unity and act of joining we often call love. My affair with our long-time lover, Earth, is apparent. You can step with me from the old paradigm into the new and you can see the tiny piece I've been given to transmute. I think you'll recognize it. If I wax pedadantic just smile and say, "Oh, he's talking to himself again."

—Stewart S. Warren, Albuquerque, New Mexico

There is only one of us here, so—for you.

COPYCAT REALLY
the work I do

I watch and I listen. On my better days I witness.
Mostly I am a plagiarist—reconstructing.

Sometimes I make messes that should have been
left well enough alone. Once in while

there's a happy accident. Someone calls that
art, so for them, I am an artist.

"there is nothing luminous
about this.
they took my children."

—Lucille Clifton

The Narrow Stairwell

Pickin' Cotton Will Make You Tan
first, a tribute to two greats

Songs poured from a water jug;
   night birds on a summer breeze.
      Albert King on guitar.

Driving pitch of a mountain range;
   jaguar in the woods.
      Young Stevie Ray Vaughn.

Pickers workin' the dirt;
reason to live, permission to die.
      Stormy Monday, Texas Flood.

Loading bales by the light of night;
   three piece suit and feathered hat.
      Bluesmen share the stage.

CRY IN THE OARLOCKS

After while the road
came up to join me, everywhere
the highway west, the unfolding.

My parents caught in the war
of privilege and prejudice,
did every bit their best. Bless
their Ohio, their Tennessee and Potomac,
their corner stone of Masonry
and backbone constitution—
what it meant to them to be white.

I opened doors with a look, my shadow
long across the wide Missouri,
my song like theirs hitched
to the Westward Ho, though,
more Socialist than they envisioned.

They had time for quilts
and parlor conversation, time
as if they owned it, time
for baby raising—at first anyway.
I grew up surrounded by books,
but read science in dirt, history on faces.
I had work to do.

When those bus stop folks
shook their heads, it wasn't resignation
but the honest-to-God blues;
the disallowed, disbelieved blues.
There's a different cadence

when your music's pulled chains
across the waves.
There's a cry in the oarlocks.

They took my picture standing
in the middle of the yard—
I, in my little white shirt
and Stewart tartan, they
in their Mint Juleps and
over hand serves. Smashing.
Long before they told me it existed
I knew about hunger.

FALLING, FALLING

In the house where my brother and I grew up
there were many basements
and just as many attics.
There were darkies down below
but no dumb waiter. There was, however,
a hamper that fell through the stories.
There was everyone's version
of the firecrackers in the shoot
and of my mother's escape
with pine needles in her nightie.
There was the night
I played with matches, but the firemen found
only a smoldering board, my failed SOS.
You told me you heard voices in the walls.

In the house where my brother and I grew up
we tricycled round and round.
We played games I can't remember.
We had plaid flannel shirts with Rayon yokes.
Getting ready for school was a small ordeal,
the big ones were invisible.
We knew better than to limp in public;
we staggered despite the rule.
A town made of bricks never forgets.
I have one here in my stomach.

In the house where my brother and I grew up
the walls were thin as flesh.
We held one another, later, at arm's length.
Each will say that the other betrayed.
I could talk to you now.
I could say that we do what we do

to save the rooms that are not burning.
Everyone tries to hold up the house.

In the house where my brother and I grew up
two boys huddle
in a corner of smoke; parents explode
at either end of the hall. The older boy
has thrown a wet blanket over the pair
to keep them breathing.
Just before the firemen arrive he will jump
with a pistol in his hand.
It's a tall house and a long fall.
I always see you in midair.

BREAD CRUMBS

He threw me on the bed, hunched me
through our clothes.
He was my friend in a gulf coast town.
I squirmed free and ran,
slept in the rocks below the seawall,
sought silence and solace
at the foot of the terrible ocean.
I Shivered alone.

His '54 Ford was ten-years-old.
He was twice my age. At barely fourteen
I was not his first runaway.
We cruised the boulevard after work;
the older boy rode shotgun.
Chicken Fried Steak cost 89¢.
You got Roger Miller, Nat King Cole
and Patsy Cline for a quarter.

My second job, after we shut down the rides,
was washing dishes in a late-night diner.
I got my cheeseburger and glass of milk for free.
I was saving quarters for Egypt or Spain.
I was on my way.

Betrayal doesn't have to touch skin.
It goes to the bone on its own.
He laughed, let on with the other carnies
like he'd made me.
They were all so much bigger,
so much quicker, louder.

Dead or alive, I've outlived them all.
I've driven cars of my own
along the sand, avoided the jellyfish,
cast my bread upon the water.

"DARE DEVIL"

Oh sure, I'd play into the role:
steal the sailboat at dawn and paddle
the glacial waters of Lake Okanagan,
not a stir of wind, drunk again,
the Mounties poised for their catch.
Or swagger down the streets of Salt Lake City
on kitchen-lab drugs, playing Frisbee
with metal trashcan lids belonging to decent folk,
    watch the Temple dissolve
into an ancient Cabalistic whisper.
And dangerous stuff too—sometimes
involving the lives of others. Feats at high speed.

Underneath the bravado and attention-getting
was not only a troubled youth, but
the ragged end of America. A story
that couldn't be co-opted, but was left
to unravel in jails, psyche wards, shelters.
I thought it was all about me, and that's
what I was supposed to think.

Pay up, be their patsy, complain, but
only about the things they show you.
Am I the system now; have I lost my nerve?

Back then I was detained again and again, now
Juvi is a multi-billion-dollar deal.
They poke sticks through the bars, proof
that we're dealing with animals.
    I am the ragged end of America.
I am its flag come half way undone.
I am your daughters and your grandfathers,

your tent towns of unemployment.
I am rolling hills of repossessed homes
empty as a dollar. I am the grocery stores
leaving, retreating into gated strongholds.
I am still troubled. I am in my 60s.

I dream prosecuting Wall Street while
the Christian Right dreams the destruction of everyone—
I share their outrage and bewilderment,
but they put my loved ones on the hurting end.
Every day I attend another funeral—
    it's always America.
Where is my risk taking when I need it?

ADDICTED

Dusty had his mother's hands.
East Texas articulation
to go with lilting words, wine cups
deep burgundy beneath the pines,
references lifting with coastal fog.
He rented a wood frame
two-story garage in the middle
of a parking lot in downtown Austin.

The narrow stairwell
echoed and creaked, a window fan
    ushered summer
into the single room, light poles
and asphalt all the way to the door.
He had his mother's hands.

It was there he told me—
There's nothing as sexy
    as a little attention.
We'd been eyeing the girls
in A.A. meetings, sometimes
they'd eye us back. Sexy.
Everything was a trigger
on the gun of that first drink.

His words were solid, a pitch fork
standing against a fence,
a pitcher of water on the board.
I was in need of everything.
Newly sober and raw to the gut,
I held the world behind my navel.
So much to fear—so much to want.

I cowboyed up just like my dad.
Without a few shots to slap back,
to squelch the rumble in my gut,
I thought too much.
    No wonder
the old man kept a quart under the seat.

Dusty slid a pack across the table
so we both fired up.
Formica dinette with two chairs,
sober literature,
drip coffee on the stove—
we were determined.

He brought it up first:
his fingers were crooked stubs,
    terminated.
My mother smoked a lot, he said,
Fetal Nicotine Syndrome.
A ripple ripped through me
but I held it in without a sound.
I had my father's stomach.

Word Curious

Bunny rabbit, disciple, socks,
afternoon, highfalutin—
by the time I got here
they already had words for things.
Thoughtless meant acting
without regard for another.
Thoughtful was going out of your way
to remember someone else.

Now that I'm working on
    emptying my mind
thoughtless has a new meaning.
How in the world
did I get so many ideas?
They just came.

Thoughts came and I used them
to build it around me.
I bent them like wire,
shaped the road that I would walk
to love, to prison,
to the ways that I would be special.
Sure, I plagiarized the world,
but this is *my* creation;
    all this danger
and fragile security, this
mock freedom. Every war I fought
has been for ideas.

Snow bank, car wreck,
memoir, deception—
I have my own definitions now.

They can be fairly accurate
descriptions: repressed anger,
arctic expanse, instant pencil,
the double-speak of tax relief,
that good-for-nothing tractor.
    But something's missing,
something big...

When I first saw that rabbit
I swam in its eyes. My own fur
tingling with music to the tips.
    Our pulsing filled
all the spaces between.
We knew what we knew.

And every time was different;
and every time was the same.
There was nothing without voice,
though some mountains
merely hummed.
Afternoons were visitors
coming in on shafts of light.
Thinkrest, faluminary, gagobbly,
helpfriend, ocean-eyes, mysticosity.

I Give Them My Word

I watch them try to die
in their un-ceremonial way—no corn,
no smoke, no feathers,
    no song to send them, only
a TV, private room, strange dream drumming
'round their heavy heads.

Their leaving is long like the time it takes
a shadow to cross the desert.
When one of them finally falls,
another takes their place in the bed.
Their death is undesirable to me.
Why do they stall?

What is given gives. Even the earth
cannot keep the sun from cracking
its crust, from shining through
from the inside out.
    Even the mighty earth
cannot hold its breath.
Why would it?
And what is dying, but more giving?

Their loneliness has become their war.
Their war has become their business.
I would leave them to die
    if only they would.
Every struggle is a cry for help.
Every unthinking lie, another lonely call.
I cannot deny even this brother.
Like a volcano, I give them my word.

MIGHT STILL BE THERE

Far from the tractor and balling calves
you find a single work glove
under a dusty bench. It's worn
in the places you pulled the gate to
or swung a maddox at some stubborn root
that staked its claim on a water pipe.

That gate might still be there
and that wise but weathered barn, and
that farm kitchen with boots at the door.
That gate might need fixing,
and somebody might know your name
pulling into the yard.
You have no idea
how much they cared for you.

It was all broken down
into small pieces: feeding the horses,
picking up something in town,
saving that old sink for you
when they tore down the cabin.

It was an easy nod
at the back of the community center
and it was a flight for life
with your guts hanging out.
It was Tupperware®
and that same stupid joke every birthday.

It was worn in the places
you pulled the gate to,
stiff the way old leather gets
when it's not been worked.

The Owl Café, a Midnight Sketch

It's the kind of place where
I can shake a lot
of black pepper on everything.

Maybe I'd written one of those
half-naked nature poems in the morning,
the kind with a curl at the end
    like a gecko sunning
in the sun room of an ashram, but now
I'm interested in tattoos.
Her hair is ink black to the root.

She teases me about getting a hot
fudge sundae when I say
all I want is just a scoop.
Her breasts are petite, perfect.
If she flirts with me again, I'm buying the place.

It's not just the shiny fruit on top—
it's the swirl and the crunch
and the drips down the side.
    It slow. . . like that.
It's Friday night and I could be home
watching *X-Files* reruns.

The jukebox dives into the floor,
    starts to swing: Aretha,
rockabilly, surfer dreams.
I'm too shy to fish for quarters
so I let it swim its course—
the chemistry, the clock-melt,
the paranormal delight.

INVITATION
December 22nd, a new year

Dirty white clean sky
with shadows of hidden snow.
I am nearby. Soon
I will be close by.

I am sun-warmed rock,
a planet large enough
for two humming low, a hunter
at winter's fire.

We have met
in the looks-within time.
Come here woman,
dream with me.

UNWRAPPED
December 26th

Since yesterday morning:
fourteen sunsets and the mist
burning off to reveal

pulsing orbs,
orange striped and pearl blue,
this enormous secret room.

Your rainbow thread quivers,
husky breath and guttural love
bent backward over the moon.

I pluck all the flowers, except
your deep Danish eyes.
Every story must be known.

The day is guided; the night is wild.
We are soaked. A serpent
breaks the surface.

To Read Them—ENFJ

Some of these artists work
from photographs, and I
from the landscape
behind their eyes—erosions,
stands of timber clear cut
for survival, a shooting star
for no apparent reason.

My wife could tell you
the color of their laces,
the length of their coats.
I know them like a sonogram:
a dark spot on the image
that accompanies them,
a menorah on the eighth night,
a crane winging over the mountain.

But their words don't match.
I have to log off their channel
to see them. I've been known
to sit in the dark.

"We must continue to dance."

—Short Bull, Brulé Sioux, 1890

THE LAST SALT

DEAD HORSE EDDY

I say I have touched this river
but my hands are dry. I say
the sky here is filled with song
but my mouth is stuffed with food.

Where are the fish nibbling,
spruce needles tumbling, mud made
from the face of mountains?
Where is my life blood lover?
I knew you, or said I did,
as we swam alongside
the sun-warmed rock.
"Like a whale," I said.

Where is my whale now; where
my turtle, my sacred current?

The labyrinth of this order form
has flung me
into an outer orbit, my doldrums
in the drifting duck weed.
I swirl here.

FLOW FROM A CORNFIELD

They come to me as black teachers,
as overweight intruders, as drivers
of antique sports cars, and as women
with morning hair and the sleep
of the moon still on their skin.
They come and say I have called them.
They are none other.

We are on a teaching farm. Here
the sky is more than blue.
More or less we are moved
and are moving.
Perhaps it is no one's fault.

A man nicks the earth
with his hoe and a new volcano
fills the church to its ears.
We call it good luck or bad,
assign responsibility: sins of farmers,
whims of the gods of fire and wind,
Tonantzin, the earth
loving itself anew. Someone,
it seems, is dreaming.

My father is the intruder
but he will tell you he is
not overweight. When our battle
is done we will both laugh
easily from the inside out.

Anyone who says
they have called the wind
can ride the red flow of this village.
Your corn sleeps
beneath the fiery mulch.

Mud Nests

I'm nobody at an international airport.
The relief of it—as I assimilate
accents passing through corridors: Italian,
Taiwanese, northern Mississippi.
    I'm one of us.   It's LAX.
We're movie stars undiscovered,
rejection letters spilling from baggage.

Flirting happens—thousands of criteria
are sorted in a second, mostly anonymous.
Ask the Austrian girl, we made it twice
coming and going in Terminal 8.
    Tight jeans are in.   I study the concourse.
If I get busted I'll say I'm on assignment,
play the "writer" card.

We're reduced, almost equal. At the airport
no one smokes or carries a gun
or doesn't pick you for their team.
Like Woodstock, babies are born
    and old friends
fall into each other's arms.
A buzz, just a buzz, holds
the paper-thin nest together.

From just under 30,000 feet
I see our geometry: nests
of neighborhoods chewed and spat
by mud daubers, stacked like virus.
I don't think: I-me-my
am getting on a small jet, rather:

here we are—70 maybe—
making a wing and a thrust,
a dream in the air.
    We believe in it.

And even if I do check my mail
the make-believe of elsewhere and elsewhen
    is suspended. I'm nobody,
and for these few open moments
you recognize me in everyone.

THE LAST SALT

Two ancient southwestern cultural traditions, the Ancestral Puebloans—often called Anasazi—and Mogollon, overlapped in the Salinas Valley to produce the later societies at Abó, Gran Quivira, and Quarai. These groups had roots as far back as 7,000 years ago and were themselves preceded by nomadic Indians who may have arrived as early as 20,000 years ago. These great villages are now ruins.

In the village of Abó
buffalo gourds dry rot among clumps
of bull grass and pale asters
    where great shelves
of burnt sandstone have collapsed
into the descending ravine.
A Visitors Center: closed.
An east/west train.

All at Abó was abandoned
for want of water, protection
from invaders, stronger medicine.

I can't hear the soft talk
of the Tompiro, only
Juniper birds winging low
and the howling horn and storm
of another westbound freight.
I hear the small labored breaths
of the blue mountains
    laying down to rest.
A chatter of leaves crosses my path.
Someone wants to speak.

Disturbed birds circle
and the thin, close clouds
    echo a dog somewhere down canyon.
I'm surrounded by messengers cawing,
cawing their plaintive by and by.
I am not myself anymore, or
maybe more of who I really am.
    I am speaking now.

Everyone here is hungry and leaving—
I am too old to make the journey.
There's no shame in it,
    no argument.
The last of them disappear
below the hill, no one turns to look.
Only the still wind, the weakened
sun, some crying in the sky.

STANDING OVER YOUR GRAVE

Plant another row of prison lights.
Sound your Supreme Court and car alarm,
roll out another thousand
thousand dollar bills to buy our silence.
Have you fooled anyone?

Have you tricked yourself into believing
that you will live forever
in the shape of singular glory?
Do they love you for it? Maybe
you can outlive your children, if you eat them.

It all comes unhinged at the end of the fourth day.
At the end of your world, ours begins.
This is the lake rolling over;
this is the last twenty-one-gun salute.
This, is a handful of dirt hitting your coffin.

A Children's Story

They used to do it at night
while the children slept,
tucked in and growing
strong bodies 12 different ways—
this business of moving fences,
stealing chickens.

Defense, they said;
If we don't do it first, others will.
I always wondered why the grumps
were so tired in the morning.

Now they do it in the living room.
Funny name for a place
where children are gathered
around real-time reruns of horror.

I used to know the difference
between a real fight
and a movie.
Oh!, that's why they call it
the *theatre* of war.
I'm going to wake up now.

Sketch to Size

She sits tall in oversized everything:
her home, her throne, her body,
her truck and dominatrix.
She gathers them like Legos®,
like sticks and stones, like dolls
of straw, like *mine, all mine.*

She learned to rule the roost
when her mom hit the road.
She learned to figure
before she could speak.
Boys who like the sound of the whip
crawl to her.

When you're small and psychological,
the pleasure of bigness
is mac n' cheese and
twelve rounds in the clip.
She sooths herself best she can.
She'd fix them all, if only she could.

Somewhere in her room
is a little pony.

MYSELF SO REGULAR

Now she's a yogi, now a princess, now
  a touch of Halloween without the blood.
  The magazine she brought to the table
  has her picture on the cover, her next identity.

Shh, not too loud—she may be listening.
  She's pineapple-upside-down cake
  for breakfast. Her deep hello is a little. . .
  abrupt. Meds?

Those neon pink librarian glasses
  match nothing. She's wiggling
  her painted toes in my direction.
  Crazy people scare me.

Sometimes when I use to think
  I was somebody—you know—normal,
  I'd push people like her out of my way.
  It's a thin line inside.

WORK, AS IT WERE

I won't lie to you—
there's something about it
that never, really, was work.
Not when we did it side by side.

The sweat dripping from my long,
blonde, twenty-year-old locks;
the tension of the wire tugging the come-along
from a corner post; shitty wages;
the 12-footers we walked
across the frozen fields; all-nighters
rebuilding the generator. Sure

we complained, that shared grief
that's both salve and glue applied
between the lines of cooperation.
We worked out who went first,
how to back up a trailer
watching hands in a mirror,
how stand back
when the guys with pencils showed up.
You can say a lot with just a look.
I won't lie to you—
there's something about it
that never, really, was work.

Sometimes we'd joke
about women and their ways,
but it was rarely derogatory;
the other men wouldn't let you
get away with mean talk.
We recognized their power.

Any guy stupid enough to clomp
into the house with muddy boots
got what he deserved.
And we held the line, a line
we *expected* them to cross.
If I could tell you all the times
gathered around our lunch pails I heard
fathers praise and brag
on their strong, capable daughters. . . .

Then a foreman would swagger through
and we'd get back
to the making of America:
  "Shake a leg. Don't strain your milk;
  walk it up to me."
  "Saw man, give me one
  92 and 5—cut the line. That's it;
  now, hand me his brother."
  "Laminate it!"

We put food in Frigidaires®
and pretty things in closets,
engineered a better widget
to save more time with your whatchamacallit.
Whether we were driven
by post war frenzy or
shook our heads
at the pointlessness of it, there was still
some kind of manly goodness
deep in the muscle when we did it
side by side. This business of work,
I wouldn't lie to you.

CROSSING TOWN

I'm crossing town,
undressing in a car.
One hand on the wheel,
then the other, elbows, knees,
    nothing. Leaves
rain down like an open switch;
the curb is high and broken.
You could say I'm... running the lights.

I'm unzipping my wolf skin
along the sleeves, removing teeth,
Slovenian eyebrows.
It's all going out the window—
hoary toenails, disregard
for sheepish rules,
    a taste for the meek.
These hungry yellow eyes.
I'm doing sixty—No, ninety.
It doesn't matter now
who taught the wolf.

It doesn't matter now who taught the wolf.

I'm crossing town,
undressing in a car.
I've got DJ Tiësto cranked.
Politicians, pigeons, bloggers flutter
    up against blurry walls.
I'm removing my sheep skin,
tugging at wooly plantlets
under the dash, peeling back
those pouty lips, those doleful poet eyes.

I'm pulling the bleat
out of my throat, the pretending
from frozen joints.
  I'm taking a corner,
fluffy white costume to the wind.
But I'm not nearly naked. Not yet.
I'm crossing town,
undressing in a car.

PAST LIVES
November 2nd

After the creation of time:
the making of memory.
Logical, huh?

But it was artists
who had the most fun, inventing
the mosaic of reincarnation.

A *kilim* to take you
    like a bird
from branch to branch.

They made it intricate and
overlapping, as if multitasking
were not enough, a game
within a game.
Levels. Simultaneity.

Pick a card, any card;
the contract's on the back.
    Murder me twice
to learn forgiveness;
be my lover on every leaf.

Up until now
there was something to solve.

More or Less

It's been a couple of minutes,
an accumulation of seconds
over little more than a week,
    nevertheless,
I can feel the days getting longer.

The drone-buzz of a small plane,
the steady lapping of traffic
on the shore of our stubborn industry.
Motorcycle, crow, footfalls in the street.
I meet you in the surging,
    though I admit,
some days I tire of dreaming.

The true clock of the cosmos wobbles.
Our so-called exactitude
would break the wing of the world,
shatter the water that's shimmering
in your cupped hands.
    We gain or lose
a few seconds every day—
more or less.

More or less, you love me
    the way you love me.
I don't know if it's the day
or the night I prefer.
Each tipping tugs at my heart,
a few more tears gained or lost.

For a Time the Trees

For a time the trees
had us to admire them,
their finely veined faces
turning with the sun,

their highway throats
lifting rivers to the sky.

For a time they admired us too,
swinging there, running off
to gather shiny things,

curling up together
when evening fell.

Then, one of us left.

Then, the other.

"The first principle of non-violent action is that of non-cooperation with everything humiliating."

—Gandhi

Renewal Dirt

OCCUPY THIS LEAF

Whatever signs we carried
we carried for the work of DNA,
for the outpouring of our kind,
for the kindness that must accompany
our flowering, and justice—
what we understood of it.

Communes tucked like bugs
into the hills of northwest Arkansas, into
the Sangre de Cristos, the Lower East Side,
is where the tribe taught survival.
At Lakota and Hopi
they welcomed us with wisdom beads
dreamt forth from another sky,
eyed us with necessary caution.

We set up camp, wasted no time
dismantling the machine.
Alternative took on reverence.
It was just yesterday, my friends.
We overthrew the system
of our thinking, and thinking makes it so.
Fifteen people living in a cabin,
fifteen thousand in the park—
hunger drives us to love, love
insists on what must be done.

Look here, the trees
are pushing out new leaves,
handing us our breath.

Bernalillo, Kewa, Corn

They started running a people train
into Santa Fe. Before that
it was freight and hobos.
Before that the light on the front
found cows and suicide drunks
in sideways snow, the driving iron
pulling La Bajada,
purple Sangres in its eyes.

Fancy or not, those rails
know a washed-out bridge
like a bank job in broad daylight,
the kind that brings a country to its knees.

The peddlers of doom that lean
their machinery against the children
are only describing their own
mortality, fear of impermanence.
Not very original of them.

You have to look past the howl
of twisting metal
to see the enchantment gurgling
in patches of family corn.
How they sing the earth
to the last ember—start again.

Whatever the light strikes
is magic. Learning to see
is letting go of objects.
If I'm not a freedom fighter,
then what?

Do you forgive me
for not counting the birds, for weeping
at sunflowers among the rusted cars?

Each time we leave the station
a door opens on the other side,
the bright yellow dust of flowers
on the tracks, the engine,
here, in my chest.

In Your Folded Hands

I'm not talking about Armageddon.
Clearly, this rage of so-called democracy
    like a grass fire is coming
to the end of its course.
"Is America Going to Hell?"
was to be Dr. King's next speech
two weeks following the motel job.
So long, Martin.

The automated cops repeat:
"Business as usual—
keep moving, keep moving."
But it doesn't matter where.
It's you, the electron spinning,
that's maintaining the lights, the sound,
the register. Even your stumble
(especially your stumble)
is their calculated gain.

Scramble back and forth
across the ledger—in the red
or in the black, it's all the same.
Dead or alive, the policy on your life
is in their safety deposit box.
But what the program fears
is true silence.

Without *us and them*
the game doesn't play.
If you don't think you're better
than others, you're not on the team.
Shame on you for being a quitter;

are you color blind
     or just Anti-American?
What it fears is non-participation—
the refuge of Reality.

If intelligence is another word
for love, reality is found
in a smiling mind.
Silence, after all,
is your invisible friend.

Eventually, all distractions are one.

And what is going to hell
goes there in its own basket of thought.
     Decide nothing.
The "What if's" and "I got to have's"
like LED numbers on glass
slide to the floor, dissipate.

It's deep silence
that undoes the cord,
     a limitless resource
in your folded hands.

Only, Thank You

Like everything else, you push
the dead outside, make them wait
in the dark; like everything else,
your iron gate and marble mausoleum
are just pages curling in the fire.

See here—I have them all,
all the dead, inside.
Not one of them can fall from me.
Look at these hands, these eyes,
this language fashioned
in the forge of crawling forward.
Would you speak with the dead?
Then speak with me.

Would you ask of failures, of reasons and decisions.
Would you ask why, or how, or who?
None of this dust is new.
Your trials and shining instant, also here.
I've left a long line of skulls in the sun.

Even your stone *mano* crushing Cacao
into ritual food was made
with the marrow and breath and dreams
of underground mountains, bent fingers
of all the fallen thieves.

These flowers, these wild ranging flowers,
these fish leaping through the waves—
what would you say?
These ancestors forming as rain,
that star winking out with a bang—
what words have you for the dead?

REGALOS
for Karla at the foot of Mount Blanca

With your grassy slope dotted
with piñon and baby-whale granite,
and your floating bamboo fish
above the snowy scalloped range;
and with your glass violin tuned
to the wild *cantos* of the desert
they try to tame in town,
    but who can doubt you
beneath so much sky?

Your *ofrenda* is a scale of friends.
Any why not pour the juice
of the mountain forward; why not
go out at dawn with the bluebirds?

The stones you've placed
move at night, align themselves
with opaque moons arriving
on the songs of your calling.
    In the morning
there's so much love to make,
so many deer at your door.

He rolls chile into your bread;
    the loaves keep coming.
From this side of the Sangres
all the children, like shining eyes,
wait for your gifts with open stars.

More So

More so, she said,
describing how we become
the older we get—more
of whatever was lodged
and repeated and became
the teeth and face
of how we dance this world.

More undone in autumn;
more undone by a flutter of yellow.
More prone to wave
at passing traffic, to leave
the party before eleven.
More intolerant of distraction.
More cranky, and not just a little.

More memories of the farm.
More fantasies about sex that fade
into hopes of helping single mothers
and single fathers get good jobs.
More like the good grandpa.
More so.

More conservative, that is to say:
waste the world if you will
but *with good* and wakeful intention.
We have shaped it to fit us, now
we must evolve from the inside out.
More like the early union organizers
before the need for bread
became justification for thugs.
More liberal, more hawkish, more

ready to abandon *all that.*
More interested in principles
than talk and legislation.
More allowing of houseflies.
More delighted by homegrown tomatoes.
More so.

More interested in the migration
of turtles and formation of outer planets.
Kind, ...or more so anyway.
Belligerent, in my outrage
at blind opulence and sleepwalking.
More forgiving of our kind,
at least every other week.

More sure of myself and my next thought.
More unsure of myself and my next thought.
More full of shit than ever.

More involved with wonders of weather
than the dictates of program media.
More open to the tinkering of genetics
and the shaping of this vehicle.

More of a witness.
More likely to move on with a sigh.
More so, she said,
and I wondered at being
more *IN* love, more *OF* it.

SISTER OF THE NARROWS
a jazz number

I
You come as extinguished flame,
as wisp, flare, contour of seeing,
a jar of forgotten form,
formless.
In the city we orange orb;
we held in each other,
we rose petal updraft.
We invisible now, smoke
before our time.

II
You run the light east,
the light rail, the devil's due.
You hold your shimmering skin,
your paper thin.
There is no gorgeous here,
no logic.
The rocking horse rooster
is mute.

III
The bird looks north,
could be true north.
The bird is dark and
looks west when
you turn the page.
The bird was a preacher's son.
If this bird speaks
the needle will change direction.

IV
You can't take off
your clothes fast enough.
No one knows
where this train stops,
and the true witness has nothing
in their head, nothing
but the homeless wind.
The dragonflies have arrived.

Done from a Dream

When northern storm clouds tore
through the high sky I knew
it was not just my dream.

I went to tell the poets. Surely
they had seen them forming there,
certainly their eyes
were wide with wonder, wonder
at the world upside down,
all the people in a hurricane.

In slow motion you can see them
end for end in midair,
their orbs suspending them,
surrounding their bodies as they flail
in the sharp, cleansing wind.

I went to tell the poets.
But the poets were busy-busy
counting hits, arranging pages.
Someone misplaced my notebook, now
how will I write, what will I say?

Done—I don't have to do that anymore.
The wind has set my pages free.

Jobless I watched with unforeseen joy.
An aurora raced, erasing.

Up and Down Roundness

This up and down roundness
is my second home.
I'm halfway to where
I've always been.

Beautiful children, you
make me want to cup water
and plant seeds.
Beautiful children, you sprout

from ground thinner than air.
When we love what we love
the roundness comes.
I tend what I can.

WATER, TREE, BIRD

When a shadow has run
its course, retreating
to the base of a thing:
a mountain range, saguaro,
grown man, fence post in sand;
or travelled so far from home
it loses identity
in the far flung of space-time
the naked day and the naked night
need neither window nor frame.

Around the fire I repeat
    water, tree, sun,
    tree, water, bird. . . .
At the edge of everything
I begin again. I concern myself
with every survival, each bloom.
I am fascinated.

This thing they call death
could hardly be an end.
The bird's shadow crosses
the day of the desert, dropping
into canyons, climbing
faces of basalt, hovering here.
We carry our own dusk and dawn.
I repeat.

Renewal Dirt

In a clearing in the city
  tree roots knuckle
    along the ground.

The sky, also unabashed,
  is azure wide.
    I am received. Here

an occasional leaf
  lets go, drifts
    in a slow ellipse. This

is where I do it,
  where I stand
    and smell the earth.

"Centuries of bones,
mountains: sorrow turned to stone:
here they are weightless."

—Octavio Paz

What Need of Forever

THE FIRST STAR IS YOURS

Daubs of sunset across a turquoise sky,
   neon coming up further down the street,
     the earth tilting to sun the other end.

We sit on funky chairs in the front yard.
   There's music here—the high song
     of grandchildren bursting

into trills and resolvable catastrophes,
   the scent of summer finally done,
     falling open on dry red ground.

Jack's fiddle is mending the day.
   He's been here, unassuming, since morning
     when the moon was hot and not for sale.

Atole Knockout
for Demetria who has been found

Your Quan Yin, carved
in blonde wood,
knows the details deep
in the *bosque* of your heart.
And though the flute fell
from those delicate hands

you placed a twig there,
a branch of peace,
staff of justice. Bread
is music in the mouths of the hungry.
You feed them

from your pantry of grace.
But for four days now
you've eaten nothing
but *atole*, blue and ancient
from your family's fields—
a hunger strike for romance.

Anything you hear
could be his name, a sheet
ripping the world apart, a sound
synonymous with tsunami.
Tuesday, or some other yesterday,
you helped him look for a house,
a place you could decorate,
water the plants, breath
the same holy air.
The kitchen is yellow.

Every room is yellow;
every door is yellow;
every street is yellow, every desert,
sky, atole, tsunami.
There is nothing
for which you can pray.

WHILE THE POET READ
at Margaret Randall's performance at East of Edith, Albuquerque 2012

The mouse, like a mini car,
tall at the rump but built
for tight parking, scooted
between chair legs and planted feet.
The floor was concrete.

The poet on stage read her epic piece
about Southeast Asia—invasions
overlapping like wide leaves
torn and tossing in monsoons,
systems snagging.

We listened, listened
to the sound of skulls cracking
beneath the blaring of political slogans,
cranes looking for a landing.
The mouse turned in and out
of traffic. I turned to look;
a woman lifted her foot.

Somewhere in the warehouse, I imagined,
were babies the size of grapes,
smaller, tails like eyelashes,
eyes blinking in the jumbo darkness,
the drone of giant disregard.
Footfalls, forklifts, landmines.

Her poem asked: Where
do we go from here?
I wondered too

for I am wary of ideologies,
the manufacture of fear.
I scurry at new promises of liberation.

The audience remained, no one
screamed or grabbed a broom.
Somewhere, I imagined, a mother
returning with food.
Perhaps we begin with mice.

They Waggle Dance
for the Han Shan Project to protect the forest at Langley, B.C.

Old friend, you're not done.
The one before you
tying this page to your waist
has also come the long road,
    the way of water
and light and shadow
and ancient yearning.
You recognize one another
swaying here in the wind. Together

your feet know
the moist rock, the quilted clouds
fleecing west to east.
You both know bugs living
on your skin—both of you living
on the skin of a greater being.
You let the earth do the turning.

In the valley you hear
her brother grumbling, hungry
    and homeless,
for that is how he sees himself.
He believes in separateness,
sees his body upright
and detached, thinks himself
alone. He's forgotten
the warmth of a cold mountain.

See how they waggle dance
around you, each describing

love's constellation, coming to you
for sustenance and the food
of remembered journey.
Old friend,
you're far from done.

The Road of Us

I cannot speak of India merely
as Uttar Pradesh or Mangalore,
of America as Denver, D.C
or Rock Springs, Wyoming.
I cannot describe my twisting street
by either end, or both.
I cannot say what this day will hold.

Is it late summer or early fall;
is this the life with which I began,
and where is that beginning now?
The hammered silver of my family's pitcher
and clappered bell above the door
do not define my address
any more than 5741 Osuna Road.

In Peshawar the goldsmiths work
Roman coins into dowry rings,
and spice merchants shovel and sift
pepper, cardamom, ginger, tea.
My body is the Silk Road.

Trade here among the many religions,
sail with me west then east
in the shifting monsoons.
I take lovers, not captives. Everyone
passes through, weaves as they will.

Tomorrow I go to America.
Who knows what goes on there.

My body is the Oregon Trail, my mind
an untamed search engine.
Salmon like leaping stars,
electricity in long swooping ropes,
something wireless in the air.

Forced March

The subject of furniture came up,
of gift wrapping, Medicare,
phones, but few
spoke of peace, though
the hunger lines of their souls
extended past the wharf,
over the bridge.
I stood there too, shivering

under the shadow of the Füehrer.
Freedom seemed too big a word—
just *some bread* I thought.
The woman in front of me,
the man behind,
appeared as frozen forms
on the forced march
of our hallucination.
I thought to step out of line.

How many times had I
passed them by,
condemned the children
for scribbling on walls,
turned victimhood into justification
to coerce and threat?
Am I my only opponent?
The subject of peace came up.

House Spiders

Are they outliers, sentries
    guarding water, eggs, darkness?
        Have they been here long?

On my simple white wall
    eight pointed stars
        let the earth do the turning.

Bent-legged they sit,
    abdomens drawn up
        in quiet geometric pose.

There is much we could say
    to one another, though
        I think it my turn to listen.

Moving Along

Am I a little boat rising and falling
or the sun burning through mist?

The big-shouldered undertow
takes only names
and the bodies we believe.

Here is the sun, here is my face,
here, my east arriving, arriving.

⁊

The sparrows, dark brown,
warm and gold, hop
along the songs of rocks, beneath

the breath of the bush. They too
know that you are here.

When the wind gusts, small birds
find themselves sideways,
a little further along.

⁊

Something underneath tugs—
just skin shedding.

Some warmth in your hand
goes out into the night,
finds the mice without a mother.

Oh, how we are made ready,
how we already know what to do.

WEIRD SCIENCE OF PEACE

They say if you can live
15 more years, you can
live another 200,
and if you can make it that far,
you're out of the shell, off planet.

Already you're browsing
for parts: hips, knees, hearts,
kidneys, livers, corneas,
eyelids that fold, hair that grows.
Soon—the Feng Shui of DNA.
Who goes on?

When I say I
want an enhancement is that
Homo erectus in the mirror;
is that the same wrinkled me
from those baby pictures?
What am I in a pair of jeans?

One day diversity may
bloom itself out. Until then
the fortification of singularity
through designer ideas.
I, Me, Mine—Oh, my.
What goes on?

Hey baby, wanna do it
in bodies, on the deck, in a cloud?

We're no longer alone;
there are others you know.
I can strike you from 7000
miles away; I can feel your love
under the bombs. I touch you,
here, in our mind, the place
where we go on, continue.

Whatever I do to the least. . . . *Why*
would I hurt myself?

With Retirement—Noticing

Teeny cheeps and trills, then
yellow and beige flutters descend.
A swoop and underhanded arc
from oak to fir across the clearing.

It's easy to speak of peace
in this garden.   It's hard
to speak of peace in this garden.

There are doves (or are they pigeons)
on the opposite roof,
leaf blowers, angry cycles,
waves of propaganda on the air.
How can I hold another war, even
at the distance of evening news?

Is this, then, my loving—
this tugging the world to me,
this *Yes* or *No* that must be said
to every passing thing?

What in the world
did I think I was going to do
with all these shiny wings, these
broken sticks, crystal-quick moments,
fading wrappers?

GOODNESS

I split the old woman's wood.
Snow fell in large silent feathers.

Afternoon like a hanging tributary
found evening's fall, the dark canyon.

The last stick hit the stack. A yellow beam
grew across the yard.

In the morning: bacon, tortillas,
coffee for the unplowed road.

PALM OF THE WIND

I'm pleased with the wind today,
as it seems pleased with the leaves
that it lifts from the red maple
and dances about, tossing them

like butterflies swirling,
zooming in winter's sun.
The sun pleases too,
and I know at this elevation

I'm made for it.
I thought up some weird stuff
the other day and made everybody
mad. I thought them like that.

I wonder who they really are.
Perhaps the wind will say;
it seems to know everyone
twirling here in its palm.

The Table, Just as It Is

I've spoken of birds in flight
  and I'll speak again.
    Here is the sun

through war-strewn smoke, the voice
  timid or not, the table
    just as it is.

Things come and go: dishes,
  diamonds, ideas
    of ownership and old age.

What do we know, and who
  made up memory and time?
    I've cast my bread on the water.

This is my love—now.
  What need of forever?
    Tell me, who stands before you?

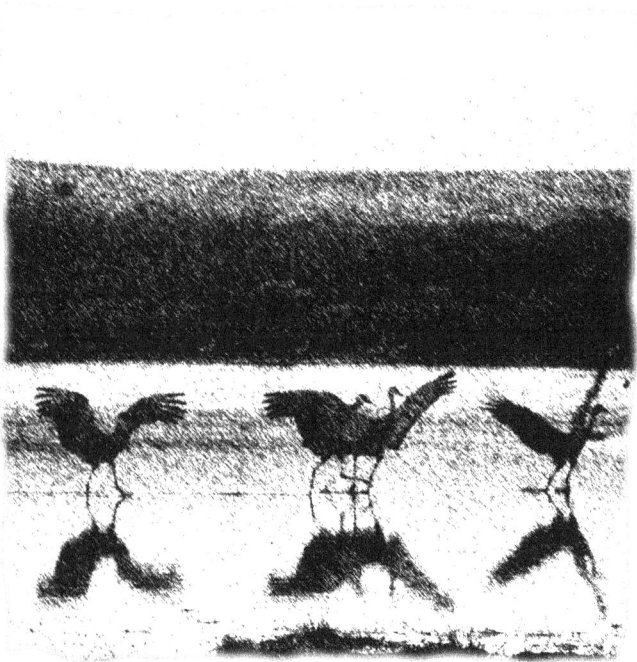

"There is nothing you have lost. I cannot tell you about other constellations because you have yet to create them. It is entirely up to you how you want to fill your heavens."

—Emmanuel

You're Somebody's Blue

STONE CIRCLE

In the circle we find the rhythm
waiting here. In the absence
of the industrial press
    we feed each other
food from our celestial bodies,
our mouths open with original words—
our beaming selves.

In the circle we turn and turn
as new growth spirals
    out from the center. My story
is not complete without yours.

Tell me about your listening heart,

about your way through the weeds,
your stumbling hunger and something
the well-to-do call boredom.
Tell me about these trees dying
here on your street, about the moon
you found in the meadow,
your sister turned away at the well.

It has all come to this, you say,
and with, or without us,
    it will come again.
You pass the talking stone to your left.

Pollinators Day and Night

Bees gone to their queen,
　　bats and moths just arrived,
　　the evening shift silent as fog
　　moving through, bloom by bloom.

Insects that sing, sing
　　in a slower-than-summer song.
　　It's early autumn after all.
　　The light wanes without a waggle.

In the morning, a few late flowers.
　　No one will be left behind
　　as long as no one is left behind.
　　Our friends keep us spinning.

STILLNESS OF AN AUTUMN TRANSIT

Having walked among the red oak
and yellow aspens of higher elevations
and the dust of first snow
on upper shelves, I settle now
into the warm breeze teasing
the still-green clusters
of ash and elm who continue
here in the valley
in their exchange of oxygen
and sheltering of friends.
A flicker flickers through.

The black crescent moon
of his family crest is upside down;
his red/orange wings
catch the sun.
The real moon, for which
we name everything else,
is of course white
when not hiding its limbs.
I'm always here when you arrive.

I could say that all other mornings
were just getting ready, but each one
was broken and eaten completely.
You might say, "All mornings are one."
Across from my small perch
an unseen songbird, a sky
without name.

Sunset at Bixby Bridge

Above a comforter of fog
we said so long
to the bald head of the sun,
red, and slipping into it.
When climbing the coast
no longer bought more time
we let it go, turned
toward the moon rising
in a notch of mountain.

Perfect in its fullness,
there was no room for disappointment,
no missing edge
on which to hang suspicion.

Evening closed quickly in the canyon
where gold-eyed moths
and the mask of goodbye
held the night snuggly
in the original secret garden.
We entered knowingly.

SPRING TIDE
from Thanksgiving it looked like this

This wave, this one
rolling in, blinding scimitar
of our age, disclosure,
deliverance, a solar wind
but not from our far flung star.

A deeper blue sent
from a deeper core,
spring tide of our galaxy, now
little more than a moon away.

The seen is cleaved
from the seer,
all that was thought to be holy
is hushed to the side.

Doors closed are open,
streets are swept, every road
rises. Where you are
is the point of contact,
every white cap
finds the shore.

Good #2

Someone on the other side
feeds me, everything
close at hand, night
wrapping around itself.

Travelling infinitely out or
toward the big crunch I arrive
in the heat of the night, the lights
coming up to call it morning.
This breath that must return, my arms
     feeling for yours
through every flowering thunder.

One man speaks of trees
with a chainsaw in his breath.
His brother sends roots
     deep
into the dark, moist rock.
They pass on the river,
frontier twins.

I know you and I am known.
     I am knowing this.
I draw upon the deck
of my desire, alternately,
to find you also there,
also, and also here.

I am every layer of mulch.
I am the problem solving itself.
Beyond this moment: nothing.

You reach through me,
    feeling forward,
my heart opening
to see how it's done.

A sister on the hill sees
the coming rain.
The crepuscular light settles soft
    over the water.
I walk with shorebirds to the end.

One Day the Sky

In the theatre I walk
with a knot, fly like a drone,
look over my shoulder.
He asks, Why did we come?
Show me what's old—everything.
Now turn, turn away.

I see the rain begin
in rivulets on the mountain;
I hear the gabble, the roar.
Flood and fire, fire and flood.
One day the sky
will be your friend.

They roar around and I
whore around with them.
Everybody's got a
leaf blower or coupons.
When the wave hits nothing
will stay in your hand.

I talk softly
past the curtain. Together
in the boat we dream forward.
They'll follow, or they won't.
One day the sky;
one day the rain.

ESSENTIAL

because it's easier to hear you laugh,
    because my body will open
        as the orchid it is, because

even the wind that batters the shore
    lays down on the dust at dusk,
        and because the moon

turns toward emptiness, quietude
    is the final tear, our essential water
        at the bottom of the well

Unknown Hour

Neither beckoning nor refusing,
the pale blue shadows shifting
in cleavages of the mountain
may know
but do not say.

Neither the wandering course
of orange and crimson trees
nor the breeze teasing
at gramma grass—not one of these
fellow companions muses aloud
at the hour or circumstance
of our leaving.

Not any of our four-legged friends
who have grown up with us
nor the old ones—
chlorophyll, silica, zinc.
Who speaks with certainty here?

We reach into the night and see
that our luminous hand
singes the precious darkness,
sends waves rolling,
bruises the perfect fruit.

We see the sand retreating beneath our feet.

Like a virus we eat our way
toward some fatal bloom;
like an embryo we morph
in restless anticipation toward flight.

Neither the desert nor the sea,
neither you, neither me.

To Be Blue

How hard the sky works:
shuffling children back and forth
in white vans and pink trains,
throwing parties on the mountain,
gathering stars for the show, saving
a little something back for moments
      when nothing
but a swatch of high wrangled blue
will set your heart spinning again.
How impossible until now.

Once in a while a leaf falls
like an open hand, steady
without the slightest twist.
You forget to be suspicious.
      You've moved
from A to Be and forgotten distance.
The idea of hugging the sky
is not so foolish after all.

Your work, too, comes easier—
tearing off a piece of bread,
      handing it
to the hand in front of you,
loving the torn leaves however
they turn in day's dream.
You see how your breath goes on.
You're somebody's blue.

About the Author

Stewart Warren, author of twelve previous poetry collections, was born in Tulsa, Oklahoma, in 1950. He hit the road early, engaging in a life of trouble making and creative expression. His poetry is both personal and transpersonal with a mystic undercurrent. As a publishing coach, catalyst and community organizer he helps others to realize their creative visions. He owns Mercury HeartLink, a small press in Albuquerque, New Mexico. *www.heartlink.com*

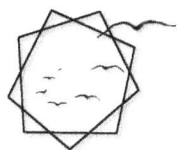

www.ingramcontent.com/pod-product-compliance
Lightning Source LLC
Chambersburg PA
CBHW051837040426
42447CB00006B/582